W9-AYA-619

RADSPORTS GUIDES

WATERCROSS

TRACY NELSON MAURER

Rourke
Publishing LLC
Vero Beach, Florida 32964

www.rourkepublishing.com

Project Assistance
Mark Denny, Managing Director, American Watercraft Association, and the International Jet Sports Boating Association, Inc., offered resources and insights to the sport. The guys at Duluth Lawn & Sport also contributed their expertise and enthusiasm...again!

Also, the author extends appreciation to Mike Maurer and Kendall and Lois M. Nelson.

Photo Credits: Cover, page 30: © Corbis Images; pages 4, 8, 11, 15, 23, 31, 33: © Vandystadt/Allsport; pages 7, 16, 22 courtesy Bombardier/Sea-Doo; page 26: © Clive Brunskill/Allsport; pages 35, 36, 37, 41, 42: © Heather Selwitz

Cover photo: Personal watercraft (PWCs) rev up the racing action on the water.

Editor: Frank Sloan

Cover and page design: Nicola Stratford

Notice: This book contains information that is true, complete and accurate to the best of our knowledge. However, the author and Rourke Publishing LLC offer all recommendations and suggestions without any guarantees and disclaim all liability incurred in connection with the use of this information.

Safety first! Activities appearing or described in this publication may be dangerous. Take a safety course and use common sense. Always wear safety gear. Even with complete safety gear, risk of injury still exists.

Library of Congress Cataloging-in-Publication Data

Maurer, Tracy, 1965-
  Watercross / Tracy Nelson Maurer.
     p. cm. — (Radsports guides)
Summary: Surveys the history, equipment, techniques, and safety factors of watercross.
Includes bibliographical references and index.
  ISBN 1-58952-278-8 (hardcover)
  1. Boats and boating—Juvenile literature. 2. Personal watercraft—Juvenile literature. [1. Boats and boating. 2. Motorboat racing. 3. Personal watercraft.] I. Title.
  GV775.3 .M38 2002
  797.1—dc21
                                2002008225
Printed in the USA

CG/CG

TABLE OF CONTENTS

Sit-down and stand-up PWCs offer different kinds of rides.

JETS THAT SKI, BUT NOT ALWAYS JET SKIS

Before you jump into watercross, know what to call the machines. You don't call every sports car a Corvette, right? So don't call all personal watercraft (PWCs) Jet Skis—even if the name fits.

"Jet" comes from the **inboard**, or built-in, pump system on this downsized boat. Powered by either a two-stroke or four-stroke engine, the jet pump sucks water into a tunnel where an **impeller** creates pressure. Pressure builds as the water flows through the tunnel and shoots out of a rear steering nozzle. This pressure provides thrust.

chapter

ONE

"Ski" comes from the idea that you can waterski without a boat to pull you. The PWC's bottom, called the hull, is shaped like one big ski to glide over water.

Only one brand is a Jet Ski made by Kawasaki. The four other manufacturers, Yamaha, Bombardier, Honda, and Polaris, use their own brand names. Fans know the differences. Riders really know the differences, just as you would know if you drove a Corvette or a Mustang.

FLOATING SNOWMOBILES

In the 1960s, Arizona inventor Clayton Jacobsen II designed a stand-up watercraft with a jet system. Bombardier noticed his work. Already famous for its Ski-Doo snowmobiles, Bombardier wanted to make a new summer machine. Engineers there worked with Jacobsen to create a sit-down watercraft that looked a lot like a floating snowmobile.

Bombardier launched the first Sea-Doo jet boats in 1968. These early one-person machines dumped easily in choppy water. Engine troubles helped to sink sales, too. The company decided to focus on its snowmobiles and stopped making Sea-Doos in 1970. Bombardier's improved jet boats didn't resurface again until 1988.

Meanwhile, Jacobsen went back to his first PWC idea. Kawasaki liked it and the company worked with him to introduce the stand-up Jet Ski in 1973.

The sport finally took off in the 1990s when manufacturers began designing jet boats for more than one rider. Today, most new PWCs are sit-down models for up to four people. Some jet boats can even tow waterskiers. Check out the boat landing at your favorite lake and you'll probably see about three PWCs to every regular boat.

MOTOCROSS INFLUENCES

Along the way, PWCs found loyal and daring riders. These hard-core pilots tested the limits of the new watercraft. They brought wild ideas from radical motorcycle races, called motocross, to the water.

With all of the fast-paced action churning up the waves, watercross has gained worldwide fans. Riders from Japan, Brazil, South Africa, Australia, Canada, France, and other countries have joined the Americans on the pro tours in recent years.

Note the similarities in equipment for motocross and watercross.

RAD TRIVIA

PWC inventor Clayton Jacobsen II was a motocross fan. He tried to invent a motorcycle to race on water. In a way, he did it!

Surf riders use the waves as ramps to launch tricks.

FULL-THROTTLE ACTION

Like motocross, watercross divides into racing and freestyle competitions. The IJSBA (International Jet Sports Boating Association) **sanctions** runabout racing for sit-down vehicles and Ski racing for stand-up models.

Racers ride laps around a closed-course marked by **buoys** in the ocean surf or on inland lakes. For example, yellow buoys show a left turn. Red buoys show a right turn. If a racer misses a buoy, he or she must loop back around it or face a one-lap penalty. Split-second decisions can determine the winner.

Another type of watercross event traces its roots to the 1920s motocross enduro that stretched across the countryside and took days to finish. Watercross **endurance** and off-shore races last anywhere from 90 minutes to six hours.

Of course, a motocross track doesn't rise up two feet or drop two feet when a stiff wind blows or the tide comes in. Waves and wakes, or water ridges trailing behind boats, also churn the watercross course. You never know what to expect next in watercross.

WAVE BASHING

Watercross freestyle competitions divide into surf and flat-water riding. Surf riding often delivers big-air tricks. Wave-bashing pilots spot their waves and use them to launch huge **aerial** moves. Flat-water riding takes intense strength to control the machines, especially pulling them up and out of the water. For both events, each pilot normally has just two minutes to throw as many tricks as possible.

Ramp jumps fall under the freestyle group, too. Just like motorcycle jumpers, PWC jumpers gun their machines up an angled ramp and fly into the air. They usually crank out a trick or two before splashing down.

BETTER PERFORMANCE AHEAD

PWCs kicked off a new watercraft technology thirty years ago, but engineers keep tweaking the machines. They focus on speed, handling, safety, power, and **environmental** impact. Cool race-car styling counts, too. To their credit, the first cup holder didn't show up until 2001.

The tweaking pays off. Pro racing models backed by the big manufacturers rip faster than 60 miles per hour (96.5 kph). The PWCs on your local lake probably top out around 40 miles per hour (64.4 kph). Some machines offer a safety speed cap on the engines to keep the machines running below 35 miles per hour (56.3 kph). Is that fast enough to have fun? Whoo-yah. And here's a tip: don't smile too much or you catch bugs in your teeth.

WEIGHTY ISSUES

Engineers watch the weight when they tinker with design. Weight affects speed and power. Dry machines start around 300 pounds (136 kg) and tip the scales at over 800 pounds (363 kg). A PWC feels light when it bobs in the water, just like you do when you float. But when the boat shoots out of the water for an aerial trick, it still weighs a few hundred pounds.

The rider's weight makes a difference, too. Riders use their weight to control and balance their PWCs, especially on turns. A heavier rider slows the machine but can control the machine better. Think of a bobber and sinker. The bobber works harder to stay afloat with a heavier sinker. Still, you need the sinker's weight to keep the bobber from floating away.

Flying off a ramp gives the rider airtime for tricks. Body position and weight help balance and control the PWC in the air.

In 1997, a British rider set the official Guinness Book of World Records top speed for a PWC at 56.68 mph (91.2 kph). Unofficial tests in 2000 recorded speeds over 81 mph (130.4 kph), but they don't count. By 2002, engineers expected a specially modified PWC to top 90 mph (144.8 kph)—hopefully with the officials watching.

POKER RUNS AND OTHER FUN

Most PWC owners ski just for fun. They tow water skiers, explore the coastline, or simply cruise to cool off. Some join local PWC clubs to meet other riders. Clubs often host a popular PWC event called a poker run.

A poker run works like a huge five-card stud poker game on water. Every PWC in the game follows a certain route, stopping at five places (usually resorts, restaurants, or marinas along the lake). Riders pick up a playing card in a sealed envelope from each stop. After collecting all five cards, they return to the starting area and the club official records the final poker hands. The official uses regular poker rules to find the winning hand.

Poker runs are usually for adults, but you might get to ride along. You know you'll have fun any time a group of PWC riders splash their "boats" in the water. So even if you haven't turned 16 years old yet, hang on and enjoy the ride. You'll get your chance to drive soon enough.

BLAST-OFF!

Have you seen little kids try on shoes? They think cool shoes make them run faster. The same thing happens when "big kids" go to buy a PWC. The truth? A rider's skill and how he or she handles risks will impact performance more than the machine.

But just like the little kid with new sneaks, you still want the right fit—the right machine for the way you ski. It's also a good idea to know what to look for when you plunk down the big bucks on a boat.

chapter
TWO

PLAYTIME PENNIES

If you're not yet 16, be thankful for the extra time to save your pennies. And, believe it, you'll need a ton of pennies. PWCs cost around $6,700, depending on whether you buy a sit-down or stand-up model with either a two-stroke or four-stroke engine. That's just the stock, or fresh-from-the-factory, machine. Racing machines cost tens of thousands of dollars.

Watch the newspaper, marine magazines, and online Web sites for used PWCs. You might find a deal. If you buy used, check for engine wear and hull damage. Inspect the **intake** very carefully. Bring your machine to a repair shop for a closer look, if you're still not sure.

GEAR TO GO

Gear up before you ski. Shop for a lifejacket, called a Personal Flotation Device (PFD), approved by the U.S. Coast Guard. In most states, PWC operators and passengers must wear PFDs. Look for a PFD that matches your weight. A Type 1 PFD, the best choice, can turn an unconscious person face up. You'll appreciate that after a wipe-out.

If you've got a brain, wear a helmet. Goggles, water shoes, and gloves come in handy, too, even for cruisers. Serious pilots wear other special clothing and safety gear, including wetsuits and leg guards.

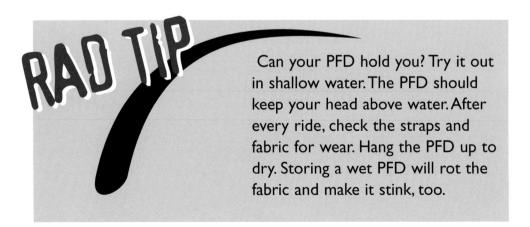

RAD TIP

Can your PFD hold you? Try it out in shallow water. The PFD should keep your head above water. After every ride, check the straps and fabric for wear. Hang the PFD up to dry. Storing a wet PFD will rot the fabric and make it stink, too.

FULL-FACE CRASH HELMET

SAFETY GOGGLES

FLOTATION VEST

WETSUIT

GLOVES

LEG GUARDS

Every PWC operator must wear a PFD. No exceptions. Try on the PFD before you buy to make sure it feels snug but comfortable.

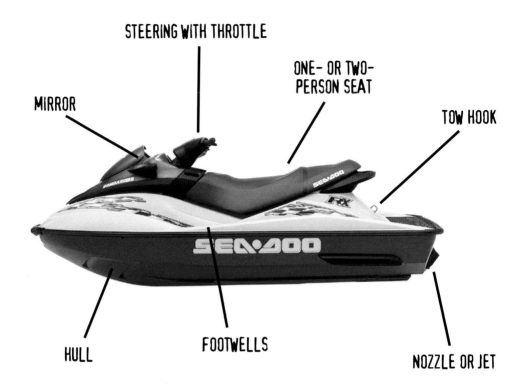

STEERING WITH THROTTLE

ONE- OR TWO- PERSON SEAT

MIRROR

TOW HOOK

HULL

FOOTWELLS

NOZZLE OR JET

ADD UP THE COSTS

Aftermarket products—the parts and equipment you add to the stock PWC—fill fat marine catalogs or online Web sites. Marine and sports stores also tempt pilots with all kinds of goodies to make a stock ride rip.

The spending spree isn't done yet. If you live away from the ocean or a lake, you need a trailer and towing vehicle to haul your PWC to and from the water. You also need a place to store the boat. Then again, if you live on water, you might need a dock or an anchor system.

Insurance and yearly tune-ups aren't bad ideas, either. Then add in the price of gasoline. PWC owners as a group spend about $300 million every year on their sport. Just about all of them think the fun of jet riding is worth every penny.

MAINTENANCE SAVES

Read the owner's manual. Really. The manufacturer tells you all the basic information about your machine, including how it works, ways to ride it safely, and how to take care of it. Create a routine maintenance check list from the information in the owner's manual. Keep track of what you do and when. Maintenance records can help sell the boat when you're ready to upgrade.

For serious maintenance and repairs, buy the manufacturer's shop manual. Work with an adult, too. In theory, you might learn something from the older person. (And you'll have someone to share the blame if something goes wrong.)

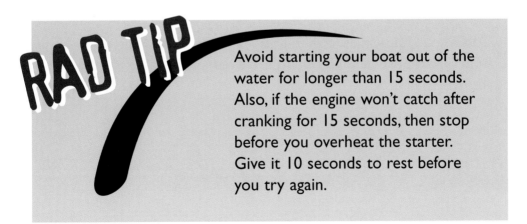

RAD TIP

Avoid starting your boat out of the water for longer than 15 seconds. Also, if the engine won't catch after cranking for 15 seconds, then stop before you overheat the starter. Give it 10 seconds to rest before you try again.

CHECK THIS, CHECK THAT

A few quick checks before and after you ride can save time and money later. They may even save your life.

Before you're ready to rip, check the

- hull for cracks
- intake to be sure it's clear
- fuel level (no fuel and the engine gags)
- oil level (no oil and the engine seizes)
- full battery charge level
- lanyard attachments for wear
- charge on the fire extinguisher (don't have one? get one)
- connections on steering and throttle cables; the handlebars should turn easily
- drain plug (you're sunk without it)

Make sure you start in more than 2 feet (.6 m) of water or the intake will suck up sand and gunk.

After you ride, use an engine-flushing kit to clean your engine. This is especially important if you ski in the ocean. Salt water eats the boat's metal parts.

'TIS THE SEASON

Winter weather means additional maintenance. Your owner's manual offers steps to take for long-term storage. Follow them. Water left inside the machine freezes, cracking hoses, cylinders, connectors, and much more. Plug up exhaust and engine outlets, too, before nasty critters move in for the season.

When spring returns, don't splash your boat without checking every part carefully. Plan at least a half day to prepare your machine for the water. And don't jump the gun. A few sunny days doesn't mean it's spring. Ride only after the temperatures stay above freezing—day and night. Cold hoses and lines lose flexibility. They crack easily then.

RAD TIP

Trailers need attention, too. Every spring, grease the wheel bearings and check the bunks and hitch for wear. Test the blinker and brake lights before every trip.

KNOW YOUR PARTS & PIECES

Can you swim? Dog paddling doesn't count. If you can't swim, forget riding. Watch the PWC action on dry land. Better yet, learn to swim.

Riding demands strength. If you ski seriously, start a workout routine that includes weightlifting and aerobic exercises. Do plenty of push-ups. Some people say you can't do too many!

Before you ride, warm up with an easy jog. Then stretch your muscles. Stretch again after your session.

REGISTER YOUR BOAT

The U.S. Coast Guard calls every PWC an inboard boat. Every inboard boat must have a Certificate of Number to identify that specific vessel. Your local PWC dealer usually has forms to apply for your boat's Certificate of Number. The law says you must show your numbers on both sides of the boat's front part.

Depending on your state, you may also need a license. Get one. Carry it onboard every time. The marine catalogs and stores sell waterproof storage bags for licenses, cash, and other essential items.

Most states require operators to be 16 years of age. If you're not old enough, then wait. Simple enough. Studies show that states with a minimum age of 16 for PWCs have fewer PWC accidents.

Connecticut, Florida, Kansas, Maryland, New Jersey, Utah, and others require operators to complete training courses. A few states even require exams similar to those vehicle drivers take. Check with the State Boating Law Administration in your state for the most current boating laws. Not knowing the laws won't fly as an excuse.

KNOW BOATING'S RULES OF THE ROAD

The U.S. Coast Guard expects all boat operators to know and obey its rules. As a PWC operator, that means you, too. Most of the laws come from common sense or common courtesy.

Some of the U.S. Coast Guard's rules
- Keep a safe distance between yourself and the other boat when you pass.
- Let other boats pass you; don't speed up or turn.
- Stay to the right when meeting another boat head-on.
- Give sailboats the right of way.
- Avoid boat channels.
- Slow down in busy areas.
- Obey signs.
- Travel at a safe speed.

THE RUDE AND THE RECKLESS

Rude and reckless riders nearly ruined the sport. Weaving, jumping wakes near boats or docks, charging at each other, exceeding no-wake speed limits, and stirring up trouble made many old-school boaters push hard for PWC bans. They won in some places. In others, local police make sure you follow the law or you'll have to pay hefty fines. In addition to the U.S. Coast Guard's rules, keep these PWC policies in mind.

Never operate your PWC:	Always operate your PWC:
In swim areas	Under the machine's weight limit
Near dams or waterfalls	Using the lanyard-type kill-switch
In a restricted area	With a buddy
At night	With a spotter if you're towing
During a storm	Wearing a PFD
After drinking alcohol	Courteously

BANG-UP BIFFS

Pleasure cruisers might get dunked now and then. Mostly, they bob back up without anything more than a cut or bruise. But wave-bashers biff, big time. They bang up their legs, heads, and back-ends. A few have even died.

Speeding and careless moves cause most of the accidents. PWC renters beware! PWC operators with less than an hour of experience, usually renters, hurt themselves more often than PWC owners. Crashing into docks and other boats, including other PWCs, topped the list of reasons for a trip to the emergency room.

TOO COOL

Most PWC riders think of **hypothermia** as a winter threat. It's actually common with water accidents. Hypothermia means your body temperature falls below normal. If your temperature dips below 95 degrees Fahrenheit (35 degrees Celsius), your body slows down. Heartbeat, breathing, and even your brain downshift.

A good wetsuit will keep you warm.

Don't wait until your speech slurs, body parts feel numb, or you pass out. The shivers are the first sign of hypothermia. Take them seriously. Get out of the water quickly and warm up slowly. Don't take a hot bath or shower. Wrap up in warm blankets and sip hot water or cider. Never drink alcohol, or you'll make the hypothermia worse.

RAD TIP

Take Funny Noises Seriously
Stay alert. Watch for floating junk and steer away. Straining, sputtering, grinding, or other funny engine noise probably means it's too late. Kill the engine immediately before you do major damage. Always, always, always turn off the engine before checking the intake.

When you fall, push
away from the PWC.

Watch for other boats when you bob back up.

DITCH IT

In the motoring world, jet boats rank among the safer options. Still, nothing on a PWC protects you from impact. And when the engine dies, the machine keeps its forward movement but you can't control the steering. Not a good scene.

When you biff, push yourself away from the machine. The lanyard will pull out the kill-switch on the engine. As soon as you surface, check for other boats. Swim back to your machine and pull yourself back on.

Studies show that PWC owners wear PFDs more often than old-school boat owners. Generally, jet boats have fewer accidental drowning deaths than propeller boats. Play safe.

RAD TIP

Pack Lightly

Think ahead when you ride. Besides your license, tuck a few essentials onto your PWC every time.
- Tow rope in case the engine dies
- New spark plugs
- Multi-purpose tool with a knife, like a Leatherman
- Marine first aid kit in a waterproof bag
- Plastic bottle of fresh water, especially if you ski in salt water
- Plastic tubing, about 1 foot (30.48 cm)
- A spare drain plug
- Signal flag (or flare for ocean riding)
- Whistle on a lanyard
- Fire extinguisher

TROUBLED WATERS

Jet boats came late onto America's waterways and found a crowded playground there. Think of all the boats people like to use for recreation: canoes, kayaks, paddle boats, speedboats, pontoons, fishing boats, air boats, and sailboats. Some people use the waterways without a boat: swimmers, fishing folks, and bird watchers.

More and more people want to play in the water, but nobody's making new lakes, rivers, or oceans. So jet boaters, old-school boaters, and no-boaters must share the waterways.

Just like at the playground, some people on the water aren't very good at sharing. Don't be one of the cry-babies. Respect other boaters and ride right.

chapter

THREE

Renting a PWC lets you try different machines. Listen to the rental shop instructions and know where the controls are.

RIDE RENTAL FIRST

Before you take the plunge into owning a PWC, rent for a while. Call the local shops and ask about places offering rentals. Your parents might need to sign papers. You might also need to show proof of your age and any boat safety courses you've completed.

Renting allows you to try several manufacturers' machines that way. Experiment with sit-down or stand-up models.

Every rental shop should give you instructions before you head for the waves. Make sure you know exactly where the controls are for each machine, and how to use them.

RARE RUNWAYS

Pilots on PWCs look for open stretches of water without many other boats around. Just like the runway at the airport, stunt riders need room to fly. If you're up to trying tricks, make sure you head for quiet water. Check with local **authorities**, too. Breaking the law can land you shore-side permanently.

RAD TIP

Start out your rental session by making about five laps in front of the launch dock. Don't go out any farther than you can easily swim back!

FAVORITES FOR FUN

Most PWC Web sites offer a page of recommended riding spots. Some of the all-time favorites include Lake Havasu in Arizona. The Colorado River and Lake Mohave, part of the Lake Mead National Recreation Area, also attract PWC riders. If you find a fine waterway with no other PWC riders, check that no bans exist. In the National Park system, four parks ban PWCs (so far). Several local lakes also **enforce** bans.

CLEAN AND QUIET

The Environmental Protection Agency (EPA) helps the federal government set standards for clean waterways. Animal and plant wildlife around waterways suffer from noisy, oily, churning boats. Air, water, and noise pollution stink for people, too.

Fuel spills from gasoline and oil top the list of concerns. Fill up on land. Catch any spills there with an **absorbent** pad you can buy at any motor shop.

Fortunately, jet boats use an impeller that doesn't hack outside the vessel like a traditional propeller. You still can stir up the bottom and make a mess for the water creatures.

- Stay out of water less than 2 feet (.6 m) deep.
- Avoid coral and kelp zones, especially at low tide.
- Keep away from marshes, home to delicate wildlife and hungry alligators.
- Leave all animals and birds alone.

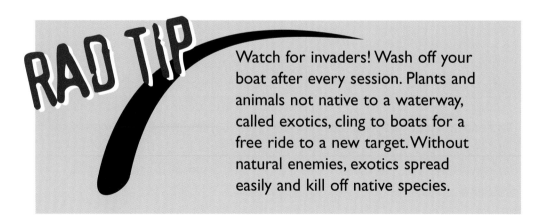

RAD TIP

Watch for invaders! Wash off your boat after every session. Plants and animals not native to a waterway, called exotics, cling to boats for a free ride to a new target. Without natural enemies, exotics spread easily and kill off native species.

LAUNCH TIME

Riders splashing around on a PWC rarely look bored. They happily zip laps for hours. These machines rev up enough thrills without adding tricks into the mix. However, a few gutsy pilots take their sessions to a new level with freestyle moves.

If you're a legal operator with a legal waterway for practicing, find a safe, experienced rider to show you the ropes. Just about every trick has a trick to it. You might catch a few hints from freestyle PWC videos, magazines, and Web sites, too.

chapter

FOUR

STICK THAT TRICK

Jet riders have adapted many of the land-based moves to the water. Motocross freestyle tricks such as heel clickers, can-cans, no-hander landers, and even the Hart attack stir up the watercross crowds.

A high flyer hanging on tight.

Wave thrashers also created some new moves that bikers can only dream about. PWCs can handle aerial barrel rolls that take the rider over onto the left or right side, under, and back up again in a full 360° circle. Deep nosedives, another favorite water trick, push the PWC below the surface and back up again. On a motorcycle, a deep nosedive is usually called a huge wipeout.

Before you try any freestyle move, remember that the pilots in videos and on TV are not riding Grandpa's tugboat. Lighter, smaller, two-person machines handle better for tricks. Also, pilots often modify many machine parts, depending where and how they ride. For example, freestyle ride plates allow more control in surf.

RAD TIP

Make sure you have a bilge pump for underwater tricks like submarines, barrel rolls, and fountains. Too much water under the hood drowns your engine.

PWCs handle all kinds of moves. Deep nosedives push the PWC below the surface and back up again.

HIGH FLYERS

Seriously, only legal and advanced riders should try to fly. Any trick can end painfully, with serious injuries or worse. Find a quiet, deeper waterway without boaters or swimmers (try for a Monday morning). Always wear your **armor**, including a helmet and even a wetsuit.

Make sure your machine purrs, too. Don't ride a wreck and expect it to dance in the waves.

Every trick takes practice. Then more practice and more practice and more practice. Start small and work your way up. Listen to advice from advanced riders. Mostly, have fun!

TRICK: TIPSY

Difficulty Level: 1 out of 5

You can't control the waves but you must control your craft. As you start building a collection of tricks, dial in the "tipsy" first for technique.

Without throttle, place both feet in the left footwell and lean your weight over. Lead with your left foot in the water while you move your right foot near the grip bump in the footwell. As the PWC tips about 45 degrees, your body dunks underwater about to the waist. Just when you think you're capsizing, goose the throttle and steer right. The front right of the boat thrusts upward. For style, wave with your left hand or splash the water. Steer to the left and level out.

The "tipsy" is a basic move that builds your control before you try other tricks.

TRICK: SUPERMAN

Difficulty Level: 3 out of 5

Nail a superman without biffing and your fans love it. Find a decent wave or wake to catch some air. You need about 3 feet (1 m) of **amplitude**, not major oxygen. Save the big air for the tough stuff. As you launch, jump out of the footwells and kick out your feet. Let them hang airborne for a second then tuck them back into the footwells. Bend your knees to cushion the landing impact.

TRICK: BAREFOOTING

Difficulty Level: 4 out of 5

Speed and balance determine your biff factor here. On smooth, flat water, run up to about 30 mph (48.3 kph). Put both feet into the left footwell while you balance and maintain speed. Step out with your left foot with your toes up. Keep your weight on the right foot until you feel comfortable. Next, step out with right foot, toes up. For style, shift your weight to the right foot and lift up your left foot. Cool. For an even cooler rooster spray, use the side of your foot and press with your heel.

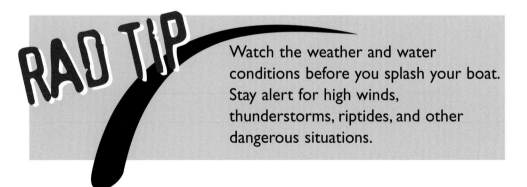

RAD TIP

Watch the weather and water conditions before you splash your boat. Stay alert for high winds, thunderstorms, riptides, and other dangerous situations.

A Superman always looks awesome. Kick your feet out and hold your position as long as you can!

*Fountains work better with smaller, lightweight PWCs that use bilge pumps.
Let the machine rest between sprays.*

TRICK: FIREHOSE OR FOUNTAIN

Difficulty Level: 4 out of 5

Fountains work best with machines that use bilge pumps. You can try it without one, but check that your bilge is completely empty. Boat size matters, too. It works better with a lightweight machine. Because you climb onto the hood backward, a smaller PWC lets you turn and hop over the handlebars.

Watch where you're headed! Follow a straight line at about 20 mph (32.2 kph). Lay off the throttle and shift your weight to the front. This kicks the back end up. Trigger the throttle to keep the nose down and the spray up.

Too many fountains and your machine gags. Watch how long you hold the nose down and let water into the hull. Give the engine a good long break between sprays.

TRICK: BARREL ROLL

Difficulty Level: 5 out of 5

The only way to make the barrel roll more difficult is to stick it in the air. Usually, it's done underwater like a kayak. Either way, you need steel nerves. Most people panic when they pull a 300-pound (136-kg) machine over on top of themselves. Before you try it, be sure you and your machine are up to it.

Some experts recommend starting with a log roll. Others say to start with a 180° spin. (If you can't do either one, you're not ready for a barrel roll.)

Find a decent wave or wake for your launch pad. Crank the handlebar left just before you leave the crest. When you're up, put both feet in the left footwell, take in a huge breath of air, and tip over. Hold on! You drill into the water and the boat hangs upside down over you. Kick out your feet and muscle the boat upright, turning a complete revolution. Rip the throttle as you come up and ride it out.

The barrel roll always stokes the crowds! Only advanced riders should try barrel rolls.

GRAVITY? WHAT GRAVITY?

You might already worship the water that Canadian Eric "Rad Rick" Roy rides over. A lot of people do. He created many of the sport's tricks, including the sick Rickter Invert. He has won more than four national titles and two world titles. Rad Rick now focuses on freestyle competitions, snubbing gravity for awesome aerials.

Rad Rick thinks the Rickter Invert is easier than a barrel roll. Flying off a perfect wave, the rider rips the throttle and throws himself backward to bring the machine in a loop. The PWC and pilot plunge underwater. Then the pilot guns the gas to come up—similar to finishing a submarine trick. Since Rad Rick Roy pulled the first one during a competition in 1998, a few brave (or stupid, depending on your point of view) pilots have nailed it, too.

Most advanced riders want to create their own tricks and set their own style. When you advance far enough, maybe you'll invent a new trick and name it, too.

FAN FOCUS

Rider: Eric "Rad Rick" Roy
Hometown: Montréal, Québec, Canada
Born: April 20, 1969
Height: 6'0" (1.8 m)
Weight: 185 pounds (84 kg)

WATER WIZARDS

Many sports busted loose in the 1990s with EXPN and other "extreme" sports shows on television. PWC racing started to develop fans then, too. Freestyle PWC riding shares many fans from motocross and snocross, the snowmobile version of watercross.

As the sport grew, the IJSBA helped set rules for watercross events. This worldwide organization also promotes safety, public awareness, and responsible riding. Even if you only ride for fun, think of joining the IJSBA or its sister organization, the American Watercraft Association.

chapter
FIVE

MAKIN' WAVES

The IJSBA sanctions many contests during the year, including the Skat-Trak World Championships. This eight-day event includes freestyle riding, but it focuses on closed-course racing.

The Red Bull Wave Bash and the Great Lakes Freestyle Tour showcase freestyle riding. They generally follow the IJSBA's judging standards. During freestyle contests, each rider raises his or her arm to signal the start of the two-minute session.

The judges watch each performance, giving points for
• Difficult moves
• Amplitude, or height, on the aerial tricks
• Acrobatics
• Balance
• Control
• Skill
• Originality
• Style

JUMPING IN

To start competing, spend time cruising the Web. Check out the major PCW sites, including the sponsor sites. You'll find handy information and tips about qualifying and entering contests all over the world.

RAD TIP

Yamahas tip left but not right. Read your owner's manual for pointers for your PWC. Every PWC has something weird.

Pro racers recommend that you start small. Check with your dealer for local clubs and events. Watch several races before you jump into one. Several companies offer racing classes, including BP Motorsports and Donald Morningstar's Star Racing School.

MONEY MATTERS

Competing takes determination, practice, and big bucks. Set a budget! Modifying your machine adds up fast. Always ask around before you sink money into an upgrade. Some doo-dads deliver pure hype. Put aside dollars for maintenance, membership dues, duct tape, and other necessities.

In addition to your machine and body armor (PFD, goggles, leg guards, and such), figure on spending money for entry fees, race gas and oil, and travel (hotel, gas, food). Sometimes you can share travel costs with teammates or other riders. A season for a closed-course racer entering two classes at seven regional events, including only travel and race gas, hotel, and race entry fees, can cost over $2,500.

PWC racing draws big crowds and many racers.
Expect to pay out big bucks if you want to race.

FALLING INTO FAME

Josh Lustic biffed so big that *Sports Illustrated* magazine ran a photo of his crash in the August 20, 2001 issue. His fall finally put a jet boat on the pages of the famous publication. Josh is actually very good at *not* falling. He became a Pro Freestyler in 2000 at age 19, just two years after he started competing. The Pro Watercross Tour named him Rookie of the Year.

Josh and his older brother Brad Lustic, also a PWC champion, head to the gym for workouts. They both ride motocross bikes to cross-train. He's a fan fave for his talent and his sportsmanship.

FAN FOCUS

Name: Josh Lustic
Birthday: May 15, 1981
Hometown: Melbourne, FL
Trains: Melbourne, FL
Machine sponsor in 2002: Kawasaki

PRETTY AND AWESOME

Christy Carlson, the six-time Women's PWC World Champion, ranks among the sport's top five all-time champions. She won her first world title in 1989, one year after she started competing.

Christy's pretty face shines with her positive attitude. She works to polish the sport's image and serves as a U.S. Coast Guard Auxiliary National Goodwill Ambassador for Safe Boating. She's also qualified to teach boating safety courses. In addition, she promotes Polaris products in commercials and works as an actress and television producer.

Although she isn't competing right now, she keeps in shape by cross-training with surfing and mountain bike riding. She also in-line skates, runs, and does yoga.

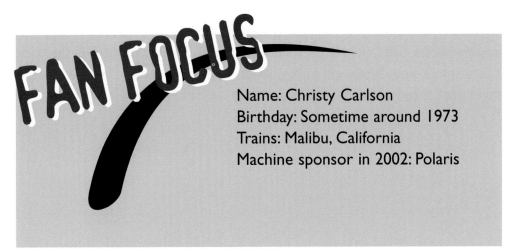

FAN FOCUS

Name: Christy Carlson
Birthday: Sometime around 1973
Trains: Malibu, California
Machine sponsor in 2002: Polaris

DRY DOCK EXCITEMENT

If you're not old enough to pilot your own jet boat, or maybe you live too far from water, or maybe long winters shorten your practice time, you can still follow the sport like thousands of other hard-core fans around the world.

Surf the Web to see the latest PWC news. Then you can see the action churning the waters off Australia, Mexico, and other places American television doesn't always cover. You can also find non-stop action on wave-basher videos.

Any of the pros will tell you that jet sports aren't about competitions. You can win or lose. You can look cool or geeky. You can dial in aerial moves or putt-putt around. For all PWC riders, the main goal is to have fun—and lots of it!

FURTHER READING

Jet Boats: A Complete Guide to Purchasing, Operating and Maintaining Your Jet Boat by Michael Kirnak. Frank Amato Publications, December 1997.

Jet Sports Magazine published by the International Jet Sports Boating Association

Personal Watercraft Adventures and Guide Book Texas: Nine Texas Adventures and Other Essential Information by Thom Bell, Thomas Bell. Life Adventures Publishing Company, 1999.

Personal Watercraft Safety by Barry Leonard (Editor). DIANE Publishing Company, reprint edition 2000.

Ships and Other Seacraft (How Science Works series) by Nigel Hawkes, Alex Pang (Illustrator). Copper Beech Books, 1999.

VIDEOS

Skat-Trak World Championships, Lake Havasu City, Arizona, from the International Jet Sports Boating Association

WEBSITES TO VISIT

www.proformancepit.com

www.watercraft.com

www.pwia.org

www.uscgboating.org

www.watercraftassociation.com

www.pwctoday.com

GLOSSARY

absorbent (ab SOR bent) — able to soak up a liquid

aerial (air ee al) — performed in the air

aftermarket (AF tur MAR kit) — replacement or add-on parts; not the original part

amplitude (AM pluh tood) — height off a jump or ramp; big air

armor (AHR mur) — pads and other safety gear

authorities (ah THOR uh teez) — people with power to make sure the rules or laws are followed

buoys (BOO eez) — floating water-traffic signals

endurance (en DOOR ans) — ability to keep going

enforce (en FORS) — to make sure rules or laws are followed

environmental (en VIH ren ment ahl) — for PWC riders, the natural outdoor elements such as air, water, and wildlife

hypothermia (hi poh THUR mee ah) — cold, below-normal body temperature

impeller (im PEL ur) — a spinning part that transmits motion

inboard (IN bord) — an engine located inside the hull of a boat

intake (IN tayk) — the place where fluid or other element is sucked in

sanctions (SANGK shunz) — makes, approves, or checks the rules

INDEX

ABOUT THE AUTHOR

Tracy Nelson Maurer specializes in nonfiction and business writing. Her most recently published children's books include the *Radsports I* series, also from Rourke Publishing LLC. She lives with her husband Mike and two children in Superior, Wisconsin.